UNDERWATER GALAXIES

UNDERWATER GALAXIES

poems

April 5 – July 21, 2004

Daniel Abdal-Hayy Moore

The Ecstatic Exchange

2007

Philadelphia

For quotes any longer than those for critical articles and reviews,
contact:
The Ecstatic Exchange,
6470 Morris Park Road, Philadelphia, PA 19151-2403
email: abdalhayy@danielmoorepoetry.com

First Edition
ISBN: 978-0-6151-4505-1 (paper)
Published by *The Ecstatic Exchange*,
6470 Morris Park Road, Philadelphia, PA 19151-240

Cover and text design by Abdallateef Whiteman
Cover collage by the author
Back cover photograph by the author

The poem *Gratitude* first appeared in Seasons, Semiannual Journal of
Zaytuna Institute, Spring – Summer Reflections, 2005, Volume 2, No. 2

بسـ_____

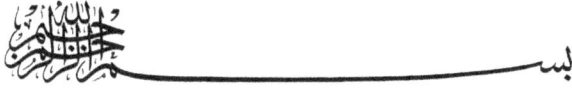

Dedicated
to
Abdurrahman and Jamila Fitzgerald,
Hamza, Nora and Kareema Weinman,
and all our hosts along the
Moroccan poetry/puppetry circuit

and to the teachers and saints
alive now and forever

Qutb Shaykh Sayyidi Muhammad ibn al-Habib
(*may God be pleased with him*)
—and the living continuation of his teachings—
Shaykh Muhammad Rahim Bawa Muhaiyaddeen,
(*may God be pleased with him*)
Baji Tayyaba Khanum, deepest pure devotion,

❖

*The earth is not bereft
of Light*

CONTENTS

❖

The eye with which I see God
is the very eye with which God sees me.

— MEISTER ECKHART

I believe,
I would like to die
with my eyes

as open
as I imagine
the only way one can imagine God's eyes
is

they are open
forever
in comtemplation

of any one of us

— CHARLES OLSON (THE HUSTINGS)

1   THE JAWS OF DEATH

I looked in at the jaws of death the other day
and found they're still full of teeth

Bouquets of roses don't impress it nor delicate sentiments
They're more like amphibious snake jaws that unhinge to take in
the whole body head to toe in one gulp and
then some

No one's ever tossed a note out or car keys at least to
let us know what's going on

Ghosts appear but they tend to be unreliable witnesses
since peevishness often seems to characterize them
or some unfinished agenda

The stable of ghost horses is always full of
restive beasts saddled for use
knocking the wooden floors and whinnying menacingly

I would reach in with a puppet and
see if death gives it eyes to see with
but I fear it might take off my arm in the process

Longboats full of ghostly serenaders by moonlight
come out to meet our colonial ship
but none dare dive in the waters for the
coins that are tossed there

Death's archipelago extends out farther than life's
and every language ever known to mankind is
spoken there

No king presides there except the king of the
One Day and every day before it and after it
all other kings find themselves elbow to elbow with
osslers and looselers hustlers and losers of every livelihood
whistling Dixie and hoping for the best

Only sanctity rings a golden bell whose reverberations
are heard in this world one wave at a time

"*Nothing to fear*" says the stranger on horseback
and the stranger sitting in the doorway
our only trustworthy informants

God bless every one of us born
that we have eyes to see where we are

and a nose for truth

and a tongue for love in the instant of its telling

4/5

2 IN THE THEATER OR BETTER YET THE CIRCUS

In the theater or better yet the circus

the elephants come out then the dancing bear then
cages on wheels with lions in them then maybe some
horses cantering prettily then usually the
clowns as many and as varied as possible doing really
nothing but seeming to be fully committed to
whatever it is they're doing

Each moment entering with spotlit fanfare and tuba-honk
hoopla the same way as in life herself if we

pay attention like the halos around each gnat in a
suspended sunlit gnat congregation

And in such glorious moments someone
ascends to a throne gets burned alive in the
citywide wildfire in Rome discovers the light-prism or
how to decaffeinate coffee

Events unheralded though prepared for way beforehand by the
Master barker of ceremonial cheer

And very dutifully the one with huge feet flaps forth
the tall skinny one holding a tall skinny mirror topples over
twenty-five in a smoking Volkswagen that goes backwards tumble
out onto the sawdust

Each of our moments on the angelic schedule takes place
precisely at that time not a second earlier or later

Especially the elephant with her sad eyes sitting on a box
or the moth-eaten lion waiting for its chance to
pounce once and for all on Roderigo Velazquez from
Venezuela in his spangley white skin-tight suit and be
done with it forever

4/6

3   THE LONG JOURNEY

I

We decided to go on a long journey

and instead the journey went on us

if that makes any sense at all

in the sense that it uncoils as we speak or
has a way of showing streets with showcases full of
furs and jewels or back alleys where some poor
soul has hanged himself all alone forever

his shadow swaying on the gravel

A shark in distant waters with its hidden overbite
lusting for blood as only in its innocent
sharkness it is capable of doing

Not that we wanted to go here exactly
wanting instead the high stellar places
stars around the head like halos with their
showering lights

But at the windows other figures appear
with lion heads or heads of geese or noises of
construction as the demolition crew quite
quietly pursues its tasks and whole
cities fall

exposing the little dusty sunlit hovels behind where real people
live with plastic cutlery and a single bowl

"I'm in the midst of it all too much to reassess"
he said or I said offhandedly

and it's true that while canoeing down the
rushing current it's hard to slow the boat enough to
accurately see the scenery

2

With or without hoods
or the collars of tremendous coats turned up around
flushed cheeks

gloves of all kinds and colors some fuzzy some
leathern with little wrist buttons some huge or
skintight

and boots clogs shoes barefoot on boats back roads
all ten toes almost prehensile on earth
in every kind of conveyance including the
fiery Hindenburg collapsing in sparks

we've traveled to our desire hoping to meet her or
him at the nether side and being in the

interim also faces completely absorbed by underwater galaxies
counting constellations and never
entirely satisfied

But lying naked and alone on a beach somewhere
fails as well

to say nothing of a crowded Tokyo subway

We would be tumbling freefall in an astronaut's
capsule over Mare Tranquillitatis hoping for
lunar hospitality

I always come back to the heartbeat for the
divinity's dwelling that then shoots its pulses
along arm and forearm even to all my

twenty fingers and toes

3

We weren't sure we were going forwards or backwards
half the time whether it was

the Ark of Noah sticking out the mountain peak's
sheer side in the
snow with demarcated animal pen outlines

or an ambiguous betterment of mankind kind of

thing where all would finally roam free of inner or
outer oppressions though as we

moved past the vaguest suggestions of boundaries
the deepest inner map of how things actually
work here emerged in greater detail

How boiling and freezing mixing and separating
action and reaction seem to operate from a

single huge cyclotronic magnet held aloft in some
divine non-material space in relation to which

everything that exists has a love-hate relationship
on the level of pure physics down to
subatomic atmospheres and out into the
tightly-packed dazzle of star-heavens

All of this taking place while we stand sipping
tea out of tiny Tibetan cups in Sikkim or

catching a taxi in Toronto with our raincoats
slick with sleet and the windows

fogged

4

The top of the earth proved to be dome-shaped or
crystal-shaped with a little stairway going up into a
doorway in nothing but a vertical rectangle of
blue light suspended over

diamond ice

into which and out of which at the same moment we
enter and exit coming totally back
into ourselves after an eyelash-long journey that

seems a lifetime

4/9-4/13

4 THE HEART TELLS US

The heart tells us to close our eyes and take the

ladder rung by rung the golden ladder that leads

upward out of the Fire

4/14

PRACTISING FOR DEATH

5

I

A small cotton wad between the teeth and
several long cut reeds from Egyptian reed beds
and an eye patch and three pairs of
good boots for the long trek and waterproof
wetsuit for the long river crossing

Yet none of these in any way useful

As well as the packing and unpacking we do
all our lives over and over

except for perhaps the ultimate thorough unpacking until there's really
nothing left no safety pins no pills against angina
no precautions at all as the great gorge

opens up before us

and only awe remains inside us

2

I've said goodbye to the daffodils out back
each one so numinous and new
such bright yellow against April's early stubble
goodbye simultaneous with hello which seems to be
our human lot on earth after all

Goodbye to zebras in the pampas grass I've never
really seen or Bower Birds from Borneo who put
colorful pink petals and dark blue cicada casings around the
entrances to their bowers to attract a mate

This itemization must go on indefinitely in all
directions at once until
mummies walk again and Saturnine planetary galaxies
unravel to their original sparkle of gestation in the hollow of
God's Hand before being flung so lovingly into eternal
night against a field of similarly flung orbs aglitter with

their own incessant salutations
hello goodbye in our blinking on-and-off universe of
compassion held in continuous suspension
by the embodiment of disembodied Compassion Himself

and that mournful cat cry in the alley out back by the daffodils
as daylight flows slowly

in giant increments

into day

3

Because we can't conceive of death really without it being
trumped by life and vice versa

Like earth without sky or water without wetness
death is life's nature like cats in cat boxes scratching the
gravel or pennies crushed flat on railroad tracks in
summer by boys ditching school

Death is life's reversible coat lining when the
weather shifts

And we'll walk carefully here in order to
run wildly there

tossing continents and armchairs into the air
our lives on ticker tapes unreadable by all but
angelic vision who shout out each
embarrassing detail with the linguistic cool of a
modern crime novelist

It's the last tablet in the Insurance Health bottle
we thought we might come across earlier but which
sits on the bottom the way a cartoon man on a
deserted island sits looking for a sign of life somewhere
even as the one tree bends down to
pluck him like ripe fruit

But we can't get used to this nearly indivisible
intimacy between death and life

That they're such close chums they can read each other's
minds and anticipate each other's actions
the Marx Brothers routine with the mirror that is only a
frame

and we're gazing right at it this moment in all its
lush colors and soft and rough textures
only in this dimensional time-frame we don't see
people going all the way back to

Adam and Eve filling the rolling golden hills each face of the multitude
distinguishable from the other
the arch criminal standing next to Florence Nightingale
the anonymous perfect saintly one just to the left there of
your mother whose face though hers looks more
radiantly ethereal than it did in life

And the sound is close to that of a night air of
crickets slowed town to deeper decibels to be an
ocean on pitch of rising and falling voices so perfectly
in tune and hauntingly beautiful the hearts of

all of us are bathed in true supernatural light

the way a baby crawls toward its mother with a
smile of perfect loving recognition so
complete it causes the curvature of the earth to
flatten for a moment to pre-Renaissance conceptions

simplifying everything into a single snap of the fingers

of firstness and lastness
life and death

miraculously combined

4/16

6 THE PROCEDURE OF APPREHENSION AND VANISHING AWAY

You have to be able to take into yourself
and then set into rows as in rows of diamonds

sights sounds thoughts word-puzzles one-touch
solutions whose touch might be single heartbeats

over a bridge on a lotus lake in late afternoon with
languorous cloud-reflections passing from shade to
deeper shade or from shadow to glittering light

and deep breathing enough to hold changeable atmospheres the way
weather changes with swoops of gusts or great
swathes of cold or heat that plow acres of rain ahead of them
or buckets of snow or nothing special

especially nothing special which is

also like rows of diamonds visited every-so-often by
very tall pink flamingos on strolls and strolling
pink flamingos are a sight too unique to slough off

or a dark green millipede fluttering along like a
purposeful eyelash on a mission nothing should divert
all experience the same
torture dramas in body-tight rooms with no food
expulsions and barefoot expeditions and slow returns to zero
even them taken in in the same way but also

expelled from the celestial showroom left to float off
in their own holy helium

God's love doesn't accept rivals or compromises

It's not an accompaniment or panacea

Those diamonds are it itself and nothing else

and the gazer on their glory and the glory itself

are the gazes He's given us to gaze on them with
until they turn to ice then water rippling away

in icily glistening sunlight

4/18

7 GOLDEN BEES

Golden bees like drops of honey with wings
appear at the open windows of our heart

It's always a bright summer day there and the
light seems to come from a non-dimensional source

Water flows in indeterminate directions and fountains
confound us with their spray seeming to go from both
the deep centers and extreme tips of their arcs

These bees bring messages from supernatural flowers
whose multicolored flames are just visible in the
nearby meadows and rolling glades
where Madame X walks with gliding footsteps
after turning back into a black swan and
then back again in her taffeta gown and downy feather train

Everything is turning back again into what it actually is
and what it isn't sings slightly off key just before
evaporating into thin air

The message from these bees with their tiny human faces
enters without sound into our heartbeats as the
flowers of their profoundest articulations blaze under a
sonorous sun

God has passed this way so often leaves still
quiver above us and stones still glisten underfoot

and everything left open to its utmost
listens as the storyteller of silence tells its
inexplicable tale to the

incessantly soothing
buzzing of these

gloriously golden bees

4/18

8   IN THE AIRPLANE HOVERING ABOVE LONDON

The plane is hovering above London

Early morning people are chattering and
lining up for the bathrooms

Dream dramas and monotonous monologs wisp above
everyone's heads dissolving into the air vents with those
midnight breaths and sleepless sighs that so
snugly enveloped us

Glare in at the side windows

Whistling whispers and lilt of talk along the aisles
mixed with ambient radio music

Rumble of jet motors as we descend

Animal smells in the antiseptic air

Suddenly everything quiet

London could be as far off as China although only
minutes away

Eternity itself could come between us

Like gnats in space held by delicate fingers

4/29

9   THE MONARCH OF THE SKY

When the monarch of the sky alights
its wings extended to its widths
the radiance that was his head
becomes a lightbulb in a lamp

on a table in the dark
in a common house on a hill
or on a flat expanse it doesn't matter

but somehow the glimmer caught in the glass
igniting the lightbulb's filament to smile
its golden glow to light the dark

encapsulating the monarch's flight
even at the highest apex of its arc
casts its light as if it casts enlightenment itself

bringing high and low to thimble-thumbed enjambment
each encoiled in each other's element

4/29

10 FIRE-EATER OF MARRAKESH

When the fire-eater put the firebrand in his mouth
the whole night sky I swear burst into flame

and when he took it out of his mouth extinguished
the night sky blackened and pulled itself tight

around us again

4/30

11 COMPLICATIONS

The complications that arise from being human
are more often than not complications we
impose on our humanity from a certain
inhumanity

The dreadful floor-and-fashion shows of history
exemplify this with utter punctuality

One man wanted to be an owl and fly
through the trees

Another wanted to eat his simple dinner

The wind that prevents them is the same wind
that pushes them on

If we knew the simplest position at any given moment
and the deep satisfaction that comes of taking it
would we bother marching with ironclad armies into
cinderblock cities?

I turn to the lamp that is my heart to search
God's Face in it

and see the silence of night

the boisterousness of day

4/30

12 TO OSCAR WILDE JAMES JOYCE SAMUEL BECKETT PAUL MULDOON YEATS AND SEAMUS HEANEY

To be a great Irish poet it seems
one must not stay long in Ireland

13 MINDSET

"A little mindset " he said to her up to her neck
in seawater

"a little mindset can go a long way"

Several universes have pulled out of their
stations and headed down the tracks since the
first articulation of that thought

he thought and brought the mirror up to her
face so she could see the elaborate transformation

Where spaces were were now radiant entities

(I get up from the composition of this poem to
blow my nose and already

old continents have drifted even a few millimeters
farther apart and the sea upon which Melville
followed his whale of uttermost whiteness

has either risen or fallen or both in just a few seconds of
first thought of breath of eyeblinks of
second and third thought-splices and the
very mindset widens that started me writing this

particular poem and no other not the one about
the three-legged zebra who outwitted the
lion intent on its kill by standing behind
zigzag trees or the

school of fish that graduated into the professional sector
and started ferrying lost fishing boats into recognizable waters
for fishnet amnesty

but *this* poem in which a lover or killer gets close to her
and whispers into her ear as she
stands in the ocean paddling in place

but I've decided not menacingly at all but actually
with heartfelt passion explaining why pursuing her across
three continents mentally and bodily absorbed in his pursuit for
all the right reasons and most honorable intentions
brought him success fully to her side in this ocean

and she looks at him with grateful eyes and
they both become in that very instant in their
lives up to that point totally grateful to the

Controller of Destinies for everything from bringing them
together here in Madagascar to the cloud formations seen

drifting past each other's heads and the pellucid blue of the
sky above and all around them and the
terns and looping aquatic snowbirds

wheeling above them and
the salt lap of ocean on their Adam and Eve bodies all these
many millennia later to the singular simplicity of their
beings and their instantaneous fulfillment

And she takes the mirror from his hand to
show him his own transformations to himself

which are somehow even more
obviously perceptible the elegance of his
yearning having made the radiant space of his
countenance even more sublime and sublimity's

ping-pong back and forth back and forth
evermore higher and higher

4/31

14 MOSQUITO LOVE-NOTE

There's that same damn mosquito that
buzzed me ten twenty years ago somewhere maybe
Mexico Morocco Spain Nigeria the

same exact one or maybe its cousin or great
aunt thrice or three-thousandth removed
buzzing around then eerily silent having

landed somewhere stealthily or waiting its chance
to drive its proboscis in

We're told by the wise not to despise even the
tiniest atom of God's creation so

"I love you!" SPLAT!

His widowed wife or fatherless child or widower husband or
grieving bereft mother now must go around for a day or two
desultorily landing and sucking blood out of

the bare necessity of its nature rather than with its

usual vampirish bloodlust though it might know in the
back of its miniscule mosquito mind that

having been born in vast quantities in stagnant
water many would have to be sacrificed especially
(though we never quite get it through our miniscule
minds) especially if we're members of such a thoroughly

unpopular species

5/1
Marrakech

15 RIMBAUD IN HARRAR

Rimbaud stood on the balcony of his house in Harrar
and squinted those steel blue eyes of his

This wasn't exactly what he'd fled France and hectically
searched for

Intolerable heat untrustworthy natives corrupt Frenchmen

The golden climes of alchemical transformation
the New Body with a New Language eluded him

This was all too real

This was the Time of the Assassins for sure

5/1

16 SILVER FOIL

for Abdurrahman Fitzgerald

Silver foil around everything

Well that's one way to preserve a certain
dead freshness

I prefer the silver foil shook like angel expletives which are
seven million percent pure that bursts out of
everything when you look then look away then

look again only with the heart shaking angelically

Each star is stripped bare that way but also
really each earth-stone each scintillant
corner of things contentedly sitting in space like

sniffing radiant rabbits that chair over there or that
forty-story building but more especially

that halo'd person coming toward you out of the crowd with a
flower-garlanded goat in his arms and a smile greater than all
Texas

All the promises you made and all the excuses

All the threats against your own person and all the
heavenly delicacies of love laid out on silver platters
each brilliantly shining also like shook foil
served to others without calculation

Until really all our existence is like a sudden
blindfold taken off in full sunlight and everything
rather than being this color or that texture is simply

Paradise bright Paradise dazzling
drenched in the colors of the pure Light
God's scattered through the universe on His

Way to Himself every silvery moment of the

day or night

5/2

17 A SINGLE HEARTBEAT

I

The fictional fire-eaters of Marrakech the Spider Lady the
Dog-Faced Boy and his wild tigers the

man-and-woman-eating plants as well as

herbal spells against both courage and cowardice

are all safely tucked in their beds tonight
under a dangling lightbulb in a house the color of
rusty terra cotta and the sky's downpours have
dried up for a moment and the chill air is
putting its own arms around itself for warmth

And we're snoozing against white pillows under
turquoise sheets and a giant red blanket here in

Marrakech where faraway echoes of dog-barks and
taxi cabs diminish and finally depart altogether in some
dark interior market-stall filled with garish pottery and
hanging mosque lamps and the donged taut drumheads of
magical nights under full moonlight

where all is as still though as slightly restless as my
sleeping wife of twenty-three years my deep-hearted harmonic chord and
Laila to my Majnun as we grow
into a single though slightly churlish tree together never far from
a laughter that resounds down the corridors of

heaven this close to heaven here as Marrakech is
where you can almost hear the living saints on its floorboards
doing the circle dance of near excruciating adoration
somewhere so nearby it's not next door so it
must be heaven after all

Paradise wherever God's lovers are sweet-tongued and
pasture-hearted bathed in a radiance so simple it looks

simply human after all and

really is after all simply

human

2

Splotched ink drops reveal worlds unseen to the
rational mind

Undersides of leaves conceal palaces of ivory green in which
chlorophilial sultans reside in latticework splendor

That vague cloud in the heavens over there unannounced by
thunder or unlit by lightning holds in its wispiness
worlds unknown and unknowable by measurement or
the usual material investigations

A nut breaks open onto Paradise

A sliver cuts through into Hell

An anonymous face in a crowd coming our way is the
first face of the universe unseen except by the
Creator directly now shedding beam after beam of
pure sunlight

A dark kitchen in any house may hold a demon or djinn just
waiting for signs of weakness

But one little light in our hearts turns back a catastrophic
avalanche and makes all its wildly cascading pebbles and boulders
stop in midair and rush in a wheeling arc back to its
source at the feet of the initial kick
of whatever devilish mountain goat began it

God help us out of numb material surrender to the usual
doorways and out the usual windows
to see Your molecularly elegant splendor always in a
new light unexpectedly shimmering

from laser pinpoint to Atlas mountain peak

The eye of the heart blinking

completely open in a single heartbeat

5/4

18 THE ROADWAY OF NO RETURN

I

On the roadway of no return
where the deer and the antelope play

and the dawn comes up in a glass of gold
and the first voice you hear is through a tunnel of
suave invisible linguistic gestures more than words
sighs in measured units of light

indications from signs as if emblazoned in neon
inside the various airy crossways of the heart

This utterly embracing road we go out on hoping for
an opening past each gate put before us in His
incalculable Mercy that are already openings beyond our
most irrational expectations

openings at the very center of things

such as that swallow's chortled cry right now
on this Marrakech terrace at sundown where I write
who's telling me something so sweetly direct only my own
thick sensual incomprehension prevents me from knowing its meaning
word for word as he swings out into the sky to
wheel and spin in the glowering sunlight
round and round with the others in mysterious
glorification's infinite circles

shedding their own comprehensively comprehensible light

2

The road that's not a road in the usual sense of
going forward down a dusty trail as new and unbeforeknown
vistas open before us

but curling into an inward outpouring or devolving back to our
first light by radiating high rings of tumult that have so
wedded us to our selves until we shake them free

or unrolling the road from ourselves our own lungs or tongues
as if rather than asphalt flowing forward a kind of
unwinding of the road of our innermost secret selves to a point in space
central to every expedition in all directions at once

Have we set out to grow old and die with a few
Technicolor adventures along the way mask upon mask taken
off us showing more and more brightly
the naked face underneath?

The sun has now gone from gold to pink above those
silhouette mountains over there and the

sunset swallows whistle their joy to the gruff sunset dog-barks
that suddenly erupt at every sundown

As the sky pastels more darkly each dwindling moment
and the promise of inner night sends its

perfumed but austere letter to our hearts

The swallow's message written there in spotlit flowering notes
as if written on staves of music to be sung

by a chorus of the sightless who make their way forward

by sound alone

3

My digital camera jammed and I thought it had
broken and then I
dreamed just now in the night that it was irreparably broken

Yesterday we walked in the covered Marrakech market in the
rain crossing mud puddles getting drenched
and that night I dreamed we were crossing a huge flood and
had to walk through raging Niagara-like waters to safety

We're in this world doing all its dramatic motions and emotions
and then we dream we're in this world

but wake up to find its transparencies are
just pictures and the light that projects them's the
key source out of cosmos out of our hearts

and we're dreaming backwards

waking up a bit more at each waking dream
each time we dream backwards

at each
new awakening

4

The driver of our van a mountain
Berber from near Marrakech
turns to our translator as he navigates the
treacherous hairpin roads of the High Rif peaks
and asks "*Would you like to know why I started smoking?*"

We noticed he often stops on some lame
excuse or other to light up a cigarette outside and often
stamps it out after a few puffs

We say "*Sure*" and he begins his tale a
man of sturdy build with coffee skin and a black
moustache handsome like a grinning actor in a B-Movie

"*It began one year ago minus two months*" he says
showing us two on his thick fingers as we
swerve past bright rain-drenched green mountain slopes and
little herds of goats and solitary raincoated goat herders

*"I'd met a young girl of eighteen — I'm thirty-two —
and we fell in love*

She would come over to my house and we'd

*talk until dawn then do our ablutions and
pray the dawn prayer together*

*We got engaged to be married and were very
happy when suddenly her father broke it off to*

*marry her to a wealthy man who worked in
Italy*

*He was a bad man who drank and gambled but he
had a lot of money*

*She protested
but he insisted*

*She called me up late that night and said 'Why don't
we just run away together?'*

*In the morning I went to her father and said
'Look I don't have much money but we
love each other very much and it'll all work out'*

Her father refused
so she got married to that man

I wept for three days

He was such a bad man and I knew
he would treat her badly

Then the man was in a car accident
in Spain on his way to Italy to
arrange the papers for her to come

and he died"

The translator's face showed amazement and he asked
again but yes the man died leaving her all alone

Our driver continued
"They'd been married only a few months but
they'd been married!

Now she was available and I still loved her very much
but I was heartbroken and she was no longer
as she'd been before when we looked forward to
our wedding and so in love

Her father came to me and asked me to marry her
he pleaded with me to marry her

I said 'No!' (his high cheekbones working and his
black eyes flashing)

'You might break it off again if a rich man comes along' I said to him

'My family would never be able to trust your family'

*Everything had changed
even though I still loved her
and love her still*

*She calls me now all the time and I
hang up on her*

What should I do?

I can't get her out of my mind

My heart is broken

I smoke to try to forget her

But it doesn't work

*I smoke another cigarette
then another*

but I still can't forget her"

"You should forget all this and marry her" we said

"Cigarettes are a bad exchange for a loving wife" I said

"Marry her and quit smoking" I said

Next day as we drove to Tetouan he seemed very
happy and excited and learned a new
phrase in English he kept repeating

"Forget the past! Forget the past!"
 He said it over and over somewhat manically

"Forget the past!"

But we weren't sure exactly
what he meant

5

On a terrace in Tangier overlooking the beehive city
right above a Moroccan McDonalds with
radio blaring bus-screech motor scooter-burble cockcrow
ship-horn blast tire-squeak and Mercedes motor-rumble
(that particularly throaty motor sound associated with North Africa)

the setting sun hitting the left sides of buildings
like yellow paint up and down the hills
in this fresh Straits of Gibraltar breeze Spain completely
obscured by 6PM mist and the light at the left in the sky
a glaring white

I think of love lost and won and the wonders of it
and its inexhaustible supply over all

how it floods each person one way or another walking along or
sitting forlorn in their houses or celebrating in ecstatic circles
under stained glass domes every moment somewhere on
earth each of us a turning facet in the single crystal

each of us an occasional wingéd landing and a
taking off again to unknown territories

having left a fluttering shadow for a moment on the open page

our original names alone surviving us

5/5-5/12

19 WHAT RESISTS ILLUSION

The sorcerer commanded the snowman
but the snowman kept on melting

The swan remembered its ugly duckling childhood
and shook its beautiful head

The cold damp room tried to be warm on its own
but inside people shivered as if in a freezer

Mice wished they were cats as they huddled in the
walls but could still hear cat-sniffs just
inches away

The water faucet dripped like a dowager with a cold
but its silver and gold fittings couldn't keep it from dripping

We see the world through glass the color of our hearts

How far away the mountain is by the steps
we think we'll need to reach it

An ancient mouth speaks wise words to us under
eyes that are dazzlingly young

Though the bodies of us bend and blow away
perfection waits for us just as we are
inside the Garden Gate of blinking lights and
absolute certainties

No place is empty of His Grace

No place doesn't even exist

A hay wagon waits under an olive tree in the sun

A white house on a hill basks in the light

Two small boys with school packs
walk through a field of grass

5/13

20 SHEEP STORY

One day a sheep got wind of the fact
that the end of its life is mutton

He tried to keep it from the others

The glorious days of spring and summer passed
as they grazed and idled grazed and grew
woollier and woollier

But he couldn't dismiss the awful fact from his mind

Though sheepish as always he tried to figure a way
out of the ultimate dilemma

Make a run for it over that hill?

Catch a bus to a distant city where he might
blend in unnoticed in his sheepskin coat?

Hunker down behind a bush until somehow the
cold fact blew over?

He was nonplussed distraught torn between
docility and rebellion

cloven

The others munched and dozed munched and wandered

He found himself doing all the normal sheepish things

He fathered some lambs some ewelets and ramlets

Was thought thoughtful by other thoughtful sheep

Was consulted by other members of the herd on
ticklish sheep matters

But the vision of ultimate mutton never left his mind

Then one day it all made sense

He awoke on a hillside covered in tiny red poppies and
golden daisies lavender and yellow yarrow under a
blazing sky the color of topaz

It was all perfect all hilly and daley all up and
down in gullies and valleys bright everywhere at once

And he noticed for the first time in the eyes of the other sheep
a something in their rectangular pupils that could only be called

contentment

only be possible with
fears of mortality abated

And he blinked and it still remained

Lowered his muzzle and munched

And it was sweet

5/13

21 HORSE OF WAR

The dog wept to see the horse
and the sky broke down

The horse of war flayed alive
and its backbone broken

Teeth enough in brutal mouths
too many teeth

The dog of life saw burning

The dog wept when he saw

The horse of war flayed alive
and its backbone broken

5/14

22 PLANE WING OVER CLOUDS

Seeing the edge of the plane wing relative to the
level of clouds

like a knife blade across foamy islands afloat on a pure blue sea

The plane wing slowly progressing as the
cloud islands pass underneath to the hiss of the
in-cabin air and the pressure on my ears as I
begin this poem not exactly sure where it's

going but confident at least that the plane is
moving forward and that London is somewhere

underneath as we begin our first leg (as they say) of the
journey back from Marrakech to Philadelphia

The plane wing's edge actually motionless to my eyes
though there's a rumbling throb and a distinct sensation of gliding

at the center of the heart where so much stillness goes
anywhere and so many foam islands pass by under it

as if we're moving forward when actually we might just

by God be expanding in the

geodesic center of His abiding Grace

5/16

23 THE FOX AND THE PHILOSOPHER

I'd love to tell the story of an old fox and a
young philosopher

sitting on a terrace at sunset discussing the world and its
evanescence

Not that I know such a story of course
nor one about three roadrunners and a penguin
or the old house that exchanged its
"u" for an "r" and got up on its four legs and galloped off into that

same sunset which is the setting of our present tale

set somewhere exotic like Samarkand perhaps with
peaches leaning in on their branches and the

philosopher picks one and peels it and eats it
while he talks

"*Perhaps*" he says to the fox whose feet stretch out beneath
brocade and velvet pantaloons and embroidered robe as he's
a wealthy fox living in luxurious splendor

"*Perhaps*" says the philosopher to the fox "*we should
consider the mere fact of our existence from a*

different point of view

Such as why you're a fox in the first place and a
rich one to boot

and I'm a poor philosopher with just a single threadbare burnoose to
keep me warm"

The fox crosses his red furry feet in his slippers and adjusts his pipe

"My dear philosopher" he begins

"you've come here over many mountains and on many vehicles
after setting out from your home passing many scenes of
beauty and carnage inflicted by some members of
one species on another n'est-ce pas?

(The fox thinks himself more cultured if he throws in
French phrases here and there)

"But did you ever see a man stop in the midst of an
action either for good or ill and say 'If I were a
fox I might not do this thing I'm about to do

or a peahen or a toro being bred for the Spanish Corrida?
I might lay down my warring arms or give out from my
fearless generosity more easily if I were a
melting snowman for example returning its
constituent watery parts to the parched earth or a

bird scattering fertile seeds in its excrement as it
hops from branch to branch or flits through the
trees? '"

The fox takes another sip from his dainty porcelain teacup
on this terrace in Samarkand

But the philosopher turns out to be a fierce hunter with a
shotgun in a forest and the fox turns out to be
hightailing it away as fast as possible
bounding under thatch and low underbrush to hide

And the hunter's thinking to himself as he runs through the
forest with his shotgun cocked to kill

"If I were a fox where would I hide?

Yet if I were a fox I wouldn't be chasing this one
but instead might be his uncle or cousin and we're chasing a
partridge or quail or peahen to eat and sit contentedly

watching a golden sunset on a hilltop together picking our
teeth clean with the

small bones"

The philosopher leans forward and breaks off a bit of
sweet cake from the golden inlaid tray set between them

"*Of course*" he continues as the fox gazes absently
out over the ancient domes and minarets of the silhouette city

"*of course in our hearts we're in one way all alike*
listening to our deepest natures and reflecting light
like moons of a single sun no matter what

species we are or what thoughts of love or rapine may
dance in our heads

The gnat as well as the leviathan have desires and
directions they go in through the air at twilight or
as they plow great oceans at midday"

The fox glances quickly at the young philosopher with his
strong beady eyes his pointed ears cocked

but it turns out the fox is circling the
man's barnyard hoping for plump chicken for supper

and the farmer is truly tired of losing his
hens to this foul predator and is waiting at the
window in the moonlight with his

shotgun thinking

"*Here we are we two*
fox and man

at each side of the fence that separates us forever from
sitting down and having an intelligent conversation
fox to man and man to fox

and I'm sure he'd have many adventures to regale my
lonely hours with and I might have a few

tips of my own to impart to him as he pursues his

foxy ways"

When the farmer catches sight of the fox in the beam of a particularly
bright moon ray and the fox realizes too late that it's

too late

and a shot rings out in the night

that echoes down the valley in Samarkand Kansas
population 204 not including the

old maid schoolteacher who drives in from the little town of Sumer

every Tuesday and Thursday

5/16
(written on the sleepless flight
from London to Philadelphia)

24 A WANDERING LION

A wandering lion who takes his taming chair with him
is better than a Dutch stool at a window with a jug of
milk on it

A tree that spreads its leafy shade over whomever comes under it
is better than three deaf girls quarreling in the wheel and cog market

A wind from the south that carries threads of tropical aromas
is better than a hacking rat cough under the stairs post-midnight

And the people who hear this
are better than he who writes it

For they come a longer way toward understanding
why the brain-shaped walnut sits so still in such a
hard shell

and who they've passed by on their way from
the luxurious horse stalls
that have caught fire and leave no survivors

All the people who sat together for eight hours in the airplane
now visible to each other as they wait at the
carousel for their battered luggage to come round

And one suitcase carries a feathery swan costume and the
score to an ancient opera in Chinese

And another is full of golden lingerie to be
worn only in moonlight after the moon becomes totally full

And another is packed with white moths waiting
patiently to come home and chew all the wool in our closets

And all the valises and bags and cases
have had placed in them unawares
an instruction manual on how to care and feed for

the wandering lion who takes his taming chair with him
as he pads down the road with his full mane glowing
and his tail swishing flies facing

an uncertain and wobbly sunrise

5/18

25 WIGS AND SHROUDS

This is a story all to do with wigs
wigs and shrouds

A merchant gets the order mixed up for a
hundred wigs to go to some revelers whose
custom it is on a full moon in summer to wear
wigs of all colors and styles as they scream and
slobber

And a hundred shrouds to go to a recent battle in the
hinterland where a hundred people some old some
young who couldn't get along wait to be buried

And an apprentice of low wit as it were
who mistakes the one for the other

The revelers are waiting with their various costumes
for the wigs to arrive
they've painted the doors of their houses black as
usual and dug a large shallow pit in the
center of the village for the dancing and
carousing that lasts until they fall in a heap

And the dead are as patient as ever though their
atoms are bidding farewell to their neighbors
as the bodies of those who quarreled without being
able to come to a just decision through compassion etcetera
begin the gradual decomposition into God's
original elements mixed together to make them

The group of revelers highly perfumed smelling sweet
the dead also perfumed with earth's rank truth
though a saint among them a twelve year old boy
exudes the odor of roses

Well the delivery is made and each to a distant
destination of three day's journey on mule back
which precludes immediate exchange

And when the revelers open the crates and find
shrouds you can imagine their chagrin

And when the townspeople open their crates onto wigs
you've got to wonder what they thought
perhaps a new theological decree has gone out they
haven't received being so remote
about bewigging the dead and burying them plunk in the
ground without shrouds

So they fit each corpse with an appropriate
wig pulling them tight around their very sad
heads framing their faces
a blond floozy's wig for the intransigent leader who
began it a curly black Afro wig for the
young one who resisted the initial injustice
and when each one is wigged except one
they begin the ceremonial burial

The saintly boy whose smile belies the
accidental circumstance of his own misfortune at
being in the way of their wrath at the
wrong time for life but at the exact right time for
death

gets the last wig an extravagant item with
silver bows and frosted waves and even a little
glass bell on top *ala* Marie Antoinette

And the revelers ready and impatient for their orgy
suddenly grow grim

The shrouds are for them and they know it
it's almost as if each one had their name
written on it

Something tells them that for them it is time to
begin to look inward

They put on the shrouds as if they are going to
a solemn occasion

They lie down next to each other in the sunset
fitting snug in the shallow pit they have dug

And some weep and wail at their wasted lives
and some laugh and sing remembering the
miraculous light they've been given

And as we leave this tale aloft in the
clouds above these two distant towns we see

The shrouded ones silent as the night closes in
some in holy dread and some bathed in beams

And in the valley a few mountains over
the dead in the ground with curious wigs on
as if where they're going requires a

wig to get in

5/20

26 A ROCK

A rock sat on its rocky pile one day
and contemplated its existence

"I may have been tossed here" he thought to
his schistose self his minute cragginess his mountainous
minuteness

"by some agency out of the blue torn from some
far rock bed or thrust up from some seismic bowels

but here I am now in all kinds of
weather presently sitting in the heat of the sun
wondering out loud to myself what I'm

doing here rather than say gathering moss down some
hill slope sitting in some serene Zen garden
stubbing the toe of someone whose toe deserves to be stubbed"

The earth suddenly shook and crashed open and the pile he
sat on plummeted a number of yards below and
so did he landing on what was his head before and
now was his base

When he caught his breath again the rock said
"It's been an adventure really
when I think of all the places I've
been in the last two or three millennia
alone!"

An ant came along and crawled up and over it

"God of rocks be praised!" he said

"I'm home!"

5/24

27 THE CLIMB REMEMBERED

In those days we used to ascend the peaks
almost without effort

(though I'm telling this many years later and the
grind of the climb may be forgotten to me by now)

We'd reach the plateau of the first palace and be
admitted into the glass hall where a serene
guardian would see to our needs and present us to he or
she who dwelt in the garden interior at the time
a place we never saw in complete daylight
even if we arrived in the morning

Later we'd pass waterfall gulches and the
ravines of lost bones until threading the
razorback ridge we'd enter the
Sonorous Zones where every sound is pin-drop precise and
bronze-bell perfect each sound enters from a deep
interior and is heard it seems from a
deep interior so that even inert things
resonate in the circles of their silences each
silence different from another

Reluctantly we'd leaves those zones and wind out of their
high valleys preferably by full moonlight
the next rise accessible only by night and it

involved tunnels in some of the hillsides and
people we'd long to see again in our lifetimes who'd
meet us there in their isolated chambers hewn from
sheer crag and precarious precipice

Some of our party would elect to turn back at
this point but they'd miss faces unlike
any we'd seen before in our lives unless those of
exceedingly wise infants

Their feasts at heights we can only imagine now
comprised of rare leaves and odorous barks and a
small black berry that utterly satisfies thirst

The next plateaus are more difficult to describe

the Lesser and Greater Chimneys of the Dove People

sudden canyons of such light we'd have to
shield our eyes light not of the
sun or moon
in which giant geodes could be
made out in the glare into which we would
thrust our faces for relief and find instead
we faced moving visions of such pictorial complexity and
subtlety I'm speechless to tell of them

And the days of our arrival are also
beyond telling since our arrival preceded us as it
were our actual arrival there at some of the
final plateaus taking place where our
usual self-apprehensions and analyses failed

echoes and a change in our blood and bones
alone attesting to the changes and if our

pores had mouths to speak would there be
words or symphonies?

Was that the Holy Face we saw?

Were those Holy phrases and long pauses between
phrases in which galaxies might slowly float
all the way from one side of the universe to the other?

I've never spoken of these things before now
and fail even now to speak of them

So let the light in my eyes be enough for you

and if you climb them take what you
see in them if you can

with you
as you go

5/25

28 A VISIT WITH MR. BLAKE

William Blake across from me sits here
insisting on whatever it is he insists on and a

great red cape opens up to show an illuminated city he says
is Jerusalem

Not quite the one over there in Palestine
but translucent walls and gates of light as only
Blake can envision

Even pinkish and silvery angels elongatedly
bending above it barely discernable in the
clouds and blowing on long glass trumpets

I look into the lively fire in his eyes those
limpid English blues of his and his

mild-mannered countenance and his almost
whispery elocution of these weighty matters in which

the whole cosmos is swept along in calamitous clouds

and he levels a look at me his right hand raised by his
face and says

"Behold the things we feared have come to pass
but the things we feared the most

may still be abated "

Black horses of smoke whinnying horribly and various
towers tumbling forward

I gaze through transparent Mr. Blake across
wispy ruins that run on for miles hoping he's
right as usual

"Shall I sing you a song?" he says

I nod and he sings in a soft falsetto of things so
elementally near they become distant as if in a

play within a play in the mind

of the Divine upraised finger of light attesting to what among
all these phantasms is real

and of the graves of the terrestrially wronged
who open their stony mouths to
sing with one voice the sweet
mercy of God and their

ultimate rectification against all forms of
injustice including tyrannies theological

and while he continues singing I can
almost see the Holy One's smile like buttery golden flakes
slowly descending over everything

Mr. Blake
your hat

the wide-brimmed felt pilgrim's hat you
wore when you first came here

Your stick
with which you touch the stars Mr. Blake
all aglitter

and the tiny chanting flames you
leave in the air

5/26

29 DEEP IN THE MARKETPLACE

Deep in the marketplace in a place so dark
no one can see much more than an

inch or two in front of his face
a man is selling something so rare it
can't be completely described and

at a price that can't be comprehended

One man thinks the price is a unicorn and
since he has no unicorn and no
unicorn exists he goes away enraged

Another thinks it means he must owe the man
everything he owns since his own ownership is
an onus on him he must own up to on his
own and this man is

closer to the mark but the bargain isn't struck

In the dark people flock but one by one
to see if they can see this thing the
man is selling

"*Is it round or square?*" one man asks
"*full or empty large or small?*"

The merchant remains silent
resiliently silent though some say they can see
light in his eyes and it flickers a certain
way to mean yes and disappears into the
murk to mean no

"Is it sea foam indistinguishable from froth on waves?
Is it amber from sunbeams that's oozed into the world?
Is it something that acts on its possessor or
something that's merely possessed?"

But the man's eyes glitter then disappear

An old woman renowned for her spiritual prowess comes
and demands it immediately at no
price at all and for a moment she
spins in place with a light all around her
and the sound of singing in the air

but she laughs in pride at her accomplishment and
sooner than it comes to her
it goes

And so it goes that people come to the merchant with
what they think it's worth to exchange for it

and some might walk away with a part of it

and others with none of it

but only the merchant himself has all of it
in the sonorous and unfathomable darkness in which it's
extended into the world for sale

Perhaps one day a complete transaction will be made
a guileless child or an old man or woman whose
heart is younger than new shoots and always
moist and green

Or a bird comes and snatches it away
or an unassuming person with no particular
image of himself or herself comes along and

inadvertently presents to the merchant what at
that very moment the merchant presents to that
person in a complete mirror image and a

perfect exchange is made

And for a full multi-dimensional instant in the depth of the
market there are golden and ruby flakes of light arising and
floating around them both out of the
center of which pours a silver waterspout of
intoxicating laughter and song intense harmonies
unheard on earth and a swirl of transparencies that

reflect all the living atoms in existence at that moment

and then it's dark again and the selection process
begins all over again

Or perhaps it's all a legend after all and no one
ever comes by who's capable of
taking on the burden of such joy

and everyone thinks the merchant has moved on
and shut down shop

But if someone stops for a moment in front of his
stall for even one unselfconscious moment

and all the conditions are right

then he appears again as always
(*he was never*
not there!)

offering the same thing at the same price

which no one has yet been able

to completely and satisfactorily determine

5/1

30 THIRTY

The number of the day is thirty

On an ocean wave in some Asian sea
a Chinese junk perhaps is being tempest tossed
and inside the cabin are thirty birthday cakes with
thirty burning candles on each one

Or in some hideout thirty boxes of dynamite are being
lined up for quick access as thirty terrorists are
strapping apparatus on that should help them
blow up both thirty locations and their
passersby as well as themselves with a
concomitant flurry of snare-drums and trumpets as
thirty gates to Paradise swing open that
turn out to be thirty fiery gates of Hell

Or perhaps more gently
thirty worms are making their way through
mud and newly turned soil to the newest
coffin lowered into the earth where a
young man of just thirty lies confused from a
fatal bullet from somewhere unexpected
as all directions from which death might be
hurtling toward us are unexpected and even
non-existent on the usual compass but

zoom-lensing into focus ultimate photo-sharp clarity
from another dimension altogether

Or thirty smiles thirty glad hearts thirty
hip-hip-hoorays thirty tosses of glasses into the air
thirty bows after a terrific performance thirty
kisses as two lovers slide their bodies closer together
down to the base of the elm tree they've been standing
under which is exactly twenty-nine feet high
and at their thirty-first kiss grows another
inch

A secret number with alchemical significance no doubt
thirty birds that go to make a Delphic Oracle
grammatically accurate

Thirty times the Name of God repeated
until the side of the mountain opens up onto
Ali Baba's treasure and the

Thirty Thieves get ten more recruits to fill out the
traditional compliment for the life-saving story

And it could go on and on such as the
thirty moves to checkmate the King in the
Rajah's courtyard surrounded by silver-clad courtiers
or the thirty pieces of silver paid to let off the

young boy from the jailor's clutches who leaves the
place of evil behind its thirty locked doors
to walk freely again in God's innumerable

breezes and ribbony sunbeams hitting his

face like a song of thirty angels
dancing ecstatically on the heads of

thirty pins to celebrate his joy

6/3

31 A LITTLE YELLOW ROSE

I

A little yellow rose grew tall among a field of
black roses

This is an unusual situation you might say and
leads us to think of the white spot on the
black bull's hide that designates the opposite held within the
very texture of *its* opposite leading to all kinds of

metaphysical niceties

But that's not what was going on here for a
gardener came by and sprayed the yellow rose
black so it would "fit in" and not
"stand out" and also if we think of the mad Duchess
he didn't want to hear "*Off with his head!*"
directed at him

But the yellow rose knew underneath it was
still yellow

So it waited until the day would come for it to
shake off its mournful veneer and shine
yellow again

But neither is this a story of conformity nor
certainly the superiority of yellow over black for example

for a Prince (why not?) rides by on his way to see his
ladylove and leans down as he trots and picks the
very painted yellow rose we began with

and puts it in his beaded jacket's lapel to
give at the appropriate moment in this

imaginary culture where a black rose signifies life and a
white rose death

But a yellow rose what does a
yellow rose signify?

The sun shone on the green meadow as the
Prince rose up to the window of his beloved and he
sang out her name and she
came to the window and he smiled with his
whole face and eyes like sparklers and she
inclined her head just so to show her
loving assent to his expression of favor

and he took the black rose and handed it
through the grillwork and she put it in her
cleavage there in the tight blue bodice of her
Romance Novel dress and he flashed a
Douglas Fairbanks smile and rode on his thoughts
inflamed with passionate focus
and passionate distraction

2

The professor rushed into the room with the
telescopic eyepiece still in his hand

He ran to the blackboard and scribbled some
equations then to a notebook and wrote them
down there as well and seemed to be
sobbing

Turned to us and said *"It's what we thought
after all"* and walked up to the board and
began explaining all the numbers letters equal signs
and other mathematical symbols he'd written there
*"The distance to the Gamma Ray burst is beyond the beyond!
Past the shirts and hoops the cavalcades and horse-shows of our
Universe past the portals and dance floors for stars and silent
stellar cemeteries out beyond the reach and within reach of the
outermost cosmic reaches and that's where they
come from like chrysanthemums of imploding
majesty into their own beating hearts having
achieved the goal of total light total unity and
total self-effacement!"*

A yellow rose in a black rose garden turning
black after ultimate yellowness

And he takes a yellow rose that same
original yellow rose out of his breast pocket
and we see his princeliness

And he puts it in his pen-holder and fills it with
water and props it on the blackboard and
we all see it

become brighter and brighter yellow until it's
no longer color but incandescence with no
clear definition until we have to
shield our eyes in that late afternoon lab

then the next moment it's dark

and the rose is black
black as night

and the equations of the Gamma burst
are complete

3

She takes the rose from her bodice and
displays it to the light who looks at it with

unmitigated delight by enwrapping it in
beams so that the black rose seems

suspended in midair her delicate fingers
seeming to disappear

So that we now have a black rose like a
vision in space appreciated beyond all bounds

by her radiant face smiling from the sole source of her
who takes it by its stem again after having

left it hanging by itself aloft
and tosses it even higher into a radiant circle

Somewhere out of our radius but orbiting us nevertheless

And by the action of this explosive self-revealing the
black paint sprayed in the first part of this poem by the
overly anxious gardener atomizes completely away and we
are now faced with a yellow rose in the night

much like its origin surrounded by black roses
only now the rose is the sun rising

and the night is almost over as it slips into
the widening slot of light like a

love letter sent by God over and over to us
as each day begins again

born among its nightly opposite taking everything

into account but truly forgetting everything in bright

fresh enumerations of its details petal by petal

and when the Prince rides by again she is both
there and not there in the window and her

head both inclines and declines to incline in his
direction so that he must begin

all over again like a yellow rose blooming among
black roses

a new rose entering the picture anew from the

rosiest black roses of night

6/8-6/10

32 THOSE WHO DREAD

There are those who dread sleep
and those who dread waking

As if Dracula were to come through the air

But the black trees that grow up in
front of us are only a woods

And the sky that opens like a cape
folds up again around a frightened avatar

Oranges on a window sill
bright as wounds

6/14

33 TO CHOOSE

To choose a sandwich or which mountain peak to
scale in a high wind takes a cunning
combination of skill and past experience an
adventurous spirit and reservoirs of daring

Or which road to go down on a sunny Tuesday with the
car radio blaring and the windows rolled down

Or which person out of the planet's six billion to spend our
lives with in the serene monotony of monogamy
on the desert island of our immediate surroundings

Or which moment to inhabit to its outermost limit
with the entire armada in full sail and rigging of our
spirit though that's not really our decision at all
and we can only hope that a few times in our
lifetimes we can expand to disappear to those
invisible horizons

Though we may choose in some inconceivable combination of
essences and forces beyond our control
which suit of clothes to wear or not wear and
which places to go to wear it

Still all of this is a mystery it isn't easy to fathom
and even our naked physical characteristics we may
not have chosen or been even allowed a preview of
which flesh color or nose-length to come

Which gender out of the myriad possibilities though our
rational pundits insist there are only shadings of the essential duo

Each breath tells us it's a new universe coming to
fruition or into focus with each exhalation

And with each inhalation everything's put on hold
in eternity's cleansing pools like a
series of canal locks in which our
soulful ship climbs up from one
water level to another in hopes of reaching

the free open sea in which all directions and
impulses become a liberated singularity

And the following exhalation
shows us that wide ocean in four-dimensional clarity

6/17

34 ENOUGH

The dark is defeated

by a sliver of light

6/20

35   RHUBARB

Rhubarb grows at the rate of rhubarb and
not at the rate of ducklings in a duck pond

Just as a cloud forms by an accumulation of
vapor changes shape every millisecond then
evaporates altogether at its own rate in an
epic setting of radiant silver among other
child cloudbanks along with a few possible
grandparent clouds still hanging around
caught in slower updrafts

But unless we watch a tendril intently as it
reaches out blind in both eyes but intensely
and sensitively searching for something to
coil round a branch a tree trunk a
strong flower stem a fence a dead body
(it doesn't mind which)

Unless we watch it unmoving we might miss its
inching along and its chortle of success when it
finally finds something

solid to wrap around

Growth unlike the angels who exist in every
fraction of their time-lapse simultaneously
takes place in a mysterious dimension that may in fact
grow along with it energized by the

beams of God's Face as they pour
into us like cascades of immortal radiation

6/30

36 GRATITUDE

He threw an arm up in the air
in gratitude

He kicked a leg out in the air
in gratitude

He moved his whole body through the air
in gratitude

He took a big gulp of rosy air
in gratitude

And his eyes shone and his voice cracked
in gratitude

And in gratitude things to be grateful for
came to him

And with gratitude dark things left him
and light things took their place

And beatitude came over him in its
luminous circles he walked through

And he moved in space with a
wider latitude

And the whole world in its various spheres
showed him gratitude

And matter mattered less as matter and
more as gratitude

A serene demeanor became his
general attitude

He opened his hands wide in the air
in gratitude

In his breast his heartbeats kept time
to the meter of gratitude

And he never took a chance with anything other
than gratitude

It carried him past the end of his
days in the same Paradise he was always in

And this is Reality
not some platitude

7/3

37 ONE-LINE POEM

I pray like a squeaking hinge

7/8

38 POEM WRITTEN ON A BOOK OF MATHEW BRADY PHOTOGRAPHS

Perhaps there's something waiting in the moonlight
to show its face

I'm writing on an oversized book of Mathew Brady photographs
pictures of Lincoln and Walt Whitman
pictures of young men and boys bloated with
arms flung back and fat legs flung forward in
death forever once in the mud and millions of
times later as people riffle the pages of books of
Civil War photographs and wonder as I do how it could have
happened and only about a hundred and forty years ago
bodies in black and white casting shadows on battlefields that are
just rolling green fields now over local hills or down
grassy valleys but then there were

guns focused out of trees on anything that moved and
yells of pain and astonishment when anyone would get
shot no doubt rebel or union yells cut short in midair
heard again now from farther away as bombs and
shrapnel cut flesh and split open organs like fruit
on streets and sidewalks empty lots and blasted buildings
in Iraq

7/10

39 BEAUTY AND MAJESTY

Don't mistake might for beauty or vice versa

The downdraft drift of a leaf

for an avalanche's downfall to a

dimple of dust

7/11

40 THE GOLDEN DOME OF THE SACRED TOMB

Lights in the distant tavern flicker invitingly
over a roaring gorge and an avalanche cataract
where many folk drown

I've seen splendor in floors of polished marble and in your eyes
O human beings almost entirely unaware of your own beauty

Seven mushrooms under a shady tree count if there are
any more mushrooms to come or if they should stop counting in their dark
mushroomy meditations

Some sea-waves arch their backs as if in various stages of outrage
others take the more peaceful route softly rolling white billows

Magdalena Ostenporra the Italian opera star gazes into her
dressing room mirror
in silence she's the same as the doorknob behind her or the
congratulatory roses at her elbow

Set out at once on the Impossible Quest
and though you may not arrive you shall be wise

A grasshopper said that first to a pebble then to a fern
then to a sparrow
the stone moved a micro-millimeter the fern wiggled its fronds in the air
the sparrow flew away

Serious discussions take place before anyone even opens their mouths

We always come back to the eyes again even in silence

The golden dome of the sacred tomb on the hill
catches every light cast by the world but itself stays golden
as each color other than its golden self
slides off into darkness

7/13

41 A TOWERING FIGURE

A towering figure towering above the heads of those who
find it hard enough now to have
any heads at all or any feet either for that
matter

And the long shadow cast the shadow in whose
silhouette outlines people live and have lived
contentedly or discontentedly for decades in the
same or different conditions altogether

And still stellar ones arise and make their mark
and sip the light fantastic and drink
God's nectar out of tulip cups

Even as the towering figure bobs and weaves like a
Macy's Thanksgiving Day Parade balloon down Madison Avenue
and the small ones call to the bigger ones for help
and the bigger ones call on God

Who casts no shadow and Who lifts the floodgates of
Light to wash over every affair however slight or trite
until we can assume responsibility for
the little compass of our acts each impulse of which
really brings on the world in the color complexion we
assign to it by our cosmetical machinations
darker or lighter as the case may be
flute singing at higher or lower registers

Symposiums of ponies!

The love that lets the leak back in that let it
bag out in the first place
all heaven let loose in a laugh or a

loud honk

I'll let you know when my eyes have quieted down to a
loud roar and glow like low embers about to
grow cold again

A life in Light
is a life well-lit

A life in darkness
considers itself lucky

7/15

42 COSMIC DANCE

The large bear dances with the small gypsy

Flat raindrops dance on the windowsill then slide sideways

Events keep dancing with history day after day

A moustache dances with the rest of the face

A bland caterpillar dances with its future gaudy butterfly

I would get up on the floor and dance right now
if I didn't think ocean surf might break over me

Twelve giraffes in a row dance stiffly with their reflections
as they stoop at a riverbank to drink

Well-dressed high school students dance with their well-dressed teachers
between afternoon class periods to an old Victrola in 1907

Airplanes dance with enemy machinegun fire
as they spiral down to earth in a last dance with gravity

These words keep dancing very deep down with silence
then this pen dances from left to right on a
blue-lined page in my notebook
that's dancing hopelessly with its own itinerant blankness

Time dances with everything in an inconceivable direction
neither forward nor upward but neither
backward nor from side to side

Greatness dances with mediocrity on a mirrored dance floor
while the petals of possibility in a Romantic atmosphere
keep falling in slow-motion through actuality's air

Endlessness keeps dancing with the right place to stop
the way a rhinoceros dances with the deepest part of a
mud hole to sink more contentedly down in to the deepest
level of its contentment

All the dancing partners in this vast universe

make an incalculable curtsy as they
suddenly change partners against the fiery backdrop
of night

As night dances with all the astronomical elements within it
even down to the flittering gnats in the air

as well as the thoughts in our heads who dance perpetually
with the longings and intentions in our hearts

who never can get enough of appropriate dance music
with which to dance with itself through the celestial veil of
crickets' voices

and this material world orchestrates outermost and most

latitudinous crescendo

7/16

43 TWILIGHT

In the twilight shade under the patio umbrella the
world shrinks
first to the size of a tiny beetle that lands on my
open book like a sesame-seed sized brown teardrop that then
becomes so still I wonder if it's napping or if it's just
hanging out for a few minutes
with a brooding human giant

Then the world shrinks to the circle of the stone-inlaid
patio table where I'm having a cup of tea and
reading *The Masnavi* of Rumi in the thick-textured
Nicholson translation
and it opens out into worlds of illuminated meaning as I
turn the page and give the stationary beetle a little
puff of air to scoot it off so it won't get crushed

and it lands on the table on its back and keeps
armadillo still for a moment but when I go back to
check on it it's on its feet again and with my
glasses off and an almost microscopic nearsightedness

see its miniscule feelers wiggling slightly up and down before
flying away
as the crazed Hungarian in the next yard
runs his motorized lawnmower for the third time today
and I pity a poor grass blade that tries to
grow in his yard cut down in its prime

as the night closes in
shrinking the world in lessening light to these

furtive scatterings of living brightness

7/16

44 WHAT POETRY IS

Sitting in the overcast living room with the front door
open and hammering and a small dog yipping down the street
reading a new book of poems I suddenly remember

my childhood dream of flying around the neighborhood by simply
aligning myself parallel to the telephone wires in the
middle of the street and just taking off by
flapping my arms but in a long smooth elegant motion

and how I loved landing on window ledges and rooftops
and flying around at ease through the blue skies of
Oakland and now of Overbrook Philadelphia at age nearly
sixty-four with the same aerial hankerings and

felt in my heart how that ability to fly is the
heart's deepest fulfillment that ease of takeoff and landing
that insouciance regarding gravity and human limitation
that airiness that sweet ability to simply

float out on a breath

which is what poetry is

7/19

45 SPELL AGAINST DISTRACTION

The little circus down the road and the
waltz class and the general ruckus all

around us try to distract us from what's
really at hand

and the guest appearance and the dowsing party
bubbles of aquariums and glittering radiolarians

in thick layers of barely penetrable distraction
and even focus itself is smithereened like confetti thrown up

But to take a break from it all and bring the
object of our heart's desire closer in closer and ever closer

to the music of leaping deer and laughing babies
the sun sliding up into day or down into nighttime

holding the Beloved's Face as close as cats' whiskers
to the muzzle of a cat and letting no

so-called emergency call us away from it
call in sick call the whole thing off call for

Phillip Morris whatever catcalls call us away
listening instead to the sound of underwater ocean currents
as they

circulate in long slow ripples through the extent of
underwater galaxies

The music of star shine the sympathetic incredible
music of love the foot pedal stuck forever in

multiple chords of harmoniousness
yearlong and lifetime rich even for

one moment's elegant elaboration on this earth

As cockcrow lights the sky in elemental pale
washes of pink and yellow against the usual dark

and the inner light of love's lanterns shines along
the esoteric trail

to lead all the late night bedazzled inebriants home

7/21

ABOUT THE AUTHOR

Born in 1940 in Oakland, California, Daniel Abdal-Hayy Moore's first book of poems, *Dawn Visions*, was published by Lawrence Ferlinghetti of City Lights Books, San Francisco, in 1964, and the second in 1972, *Burnt Heart/Ode to the War Dead*. He created and directed *The Floating Lotus Magic Opera Company* in Berkeley, California in the late 60s, and presented two major productions, *The Walls Are Running Blood*, and *Bliss Apocalypse*. He became a Sufi Muslim in 1970, performed the Hajj in 1972, and lived and traveled throughout Morocco, Spain, Algeria and Nigeria, landing in California and publishing *The Desert is the Only Way Out*, and *Chronicles of Akhira* in the early 80s (Zilzal Press). Residing in Philadelphia since 1990, in 1996 he published *The Ramadan Sonnets* (Jusoor/City Lights), and in 2002, *The Blind Beekeeper* (Jusoor/Syracuse University Press). He has been the major editor for a number of works, including *The Burdah* of Shaykh Busiri, translated by Shaykh Hamza Yusuf, and the poetry of Palestinian poet, Mahmoud Darwish, translated by Munir Akash. He is also widely published on the worldwide web: *The American Muslim, DeenPort*, and his own website, among others: www.danielmoorepoetry.com. The Ecstatic Exchange Series is bringing out the extensive body of his works of poetry, beginning in 2005 with *Mars & Beyond, Laughing Buddha Weeping Sufi, Salt Prayers* and a revised edition of *Ramadan Sonnets*, and continuing in 2006 with *Psalms for the Brokenhearted, I Imagine a Lion, Coattails of the Saint, Love is a Letter Burning in a High Wind* and *Abdallah Jones and the Disappearing-Dust Caper*. *The Flame of Transformation Turns to Light* and *Underwater Galaxies* are the first volumes to appear in 2007.

POETIC WORKS BY DANIEL ABDAL-HAYY MOORE

Published and Unpublished
(many to appear in *The Ecstatic Exchange* Series)

Dawn Visions (published by City Lights, 1964)
Burnt Heart/Ode to the War Dead (published by City Lights, 1972)
This Body of Black Light Gone Through the Diamond (printed by Fred Stone, Cambridge, Mass, 1965)
On The Streets at Night Alone (1965?)
All Hail the Surgical Lamp (1967)
States of Amazement (1970)

Abdullah Jones and the Disappearing-Dust Caper (published by The Ecstatic Exchange, Crescent Series, 2006)
The Chronicles of Akhira (1981) (published by Zilzal Press with Typoglyphs by Karl Kempton, 1986)
Mouloud (1984) (A Zilzal Press chapbook, 1995)
Man is the Crown of Creation (1984)
The Look of the Lion (The Parabolas of Sight) (1984)
The Desert is the Only Way Out (completed 4/21/84) (Zilzal Press chapbook, 1985)
Atomic Dance (1984) (am here books, 1988)
Outlandish Tales (1984)
Awake as Never Before (12/26/84) (Zilzal Press chapbook, 1993)
Glorious Intervals (1/1/85) (Zilzal Press chapbook, ?)
Long Days on Earth/Book I (1/28 – 8/30/85)
Long Days on Earth/Book II (Hayy Ibn Yaqzan)
Long Days on Earth/Book III (1/22/86)
Long Days on Earth/Book IV (1986)
The Ramadan Sonnets (Long Days on Earth/Book V) (5/9 – 6/11/86) (Published by Jusoor/City Lights Books, 1996) (Republished as **Ramadan Sonnets** by The Ecstatic Exchange 2005)
Long Days on Earth/Book VI (6-8/30/86)
Holograms (9/4/86 – 3/26/87)
History of the World (The Epic of Man's Survival) (4/7 – 6/18/87)
Exploratory Odes (6/25 – 10/18/87)
The Man at the End of the World (11/11 – 12/10/87)
The Perfect Orchestra (3/30 – 7/25/88)
Fed from Underground Springs (7/30 – 11/23/88)
Ideas of the Heart (11/27/88 – 5/5/89)
New Poems (scattered poems, out of series, from 3/24 – 8/9/89)
Facing Mecca (5/16 – 11/11/89)
A Maddening Disregard for the Passage of Time (11/17/89 – 5/20/90)

The Heart Falls in Love with Visions of Perfection (6/15/90 – 6/2/91)
Like When You Wave at a Train and the Train Hoots Back at You (Farid's Book) (6/11 –
7/26/91)
Orpheus Meets Morpheus (8/1/91– 3/14/92)
The Puzzle (3/21/92 – 8/17/93)
The Greater Vehicle (10/17/93 – 4/30/94)
A Hundred Little 3-D Pictures (5/14/94 – 9/11/95)
The Angel Broadcast (9/29 – 12/17/95)
Mecca/Medina Time-Warp (12/19/95 – 1/6/96) (Published as a Zilzal Press chapbook, 1996)
Miracle Songs for the Millennium (1/20 – 10/16/96)
The Blind Beekeeper (11/15/96 – 5/30/97) (Published 2002 by Jusoor/Syracuse University
Press)
Chants for the Beauty Feast (6/3 – 10/28/97)
Open Doors (10/29/97 – 5/23/98)
Salt Prayers (5/29 – 10/24/98) (Published by The Ecstatic Exchange, 2005)
Some (10/25/98 – 4/25/99)
Flight to Egypt (5/1 – 5/16/99)
I Imagine a Lion (5/21 – 11/15/99) (Published by The Ecstatic Exchange, 2006)
Millennial Prognostications (11/25/99 – 2/2/2000)
The Book of Infinite Beauty (2/4 – 10/8/2000)
Blood Songs (10/9/2000 – 4/3/2001)
The Music Space (4/10 – 9/16/2001)
Where Death Goes (9/20/2001 – 5/1/2002)
The Flame of Transformation Turns to Light (99 Ghazals Written in English) (5/14 – 8/21/
2002) (Published by The Ecstatic Exchange, 2007)
Through Rose-Colored Glasses (7/22/2002 – 1/15/2003)
Psalms for the Broken-Hearted (1/22 – 5/25/2003) (Published by The Ecstatic Exchange,
2006)
Hoopoe's Argument (5/27 – 9/18/03)
Love is a Letter Burning in a High Wind (9/21 – 11/6/2003) (Published by The Ecstatic
Exchange, 2006)
Laughing Buddha/Weeping Sufi (11/7/2003 – 1/10/2004) (Published by The Ecstatic
Exchange, 2005)
Mars and Beyond (1/20 – 3/29/2004) (Published by The Ecstatic Exchange, 2005)
Underwater Galaxies (4/5 – 7/21/2004) (Published by The Ecstatic Exchange, 2007)
Cooked Oranges (7/23/2004 – 1/24/2005)
Holiday from the Perfect Crime (1/25 – 6/11/2005)
Stories Too Fiery to Sing Too Watery to Whisper (6/13 – 10/24/2005)
Coattails of the Saint (10/26/2005 – 5/10/2006)
In the Realm of Neither (5/14/2006 – 11/12/06)
Invention of the Wheel (11/13/06 –)

www.ingramcontent.com/pod-product-compliance
Lightning Source LLC
Chambersburg PA
CBHW020916090426
42736CB00008B/659